This Book Belongs To

_____

This Book Is About My

_____

This Book Was Given To Me By

_____

# when a
# *Grandparent*
## dies

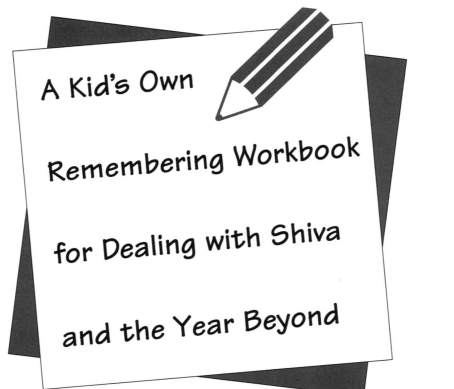

A Kid's Own

Remembering Workbook

for Dealing with Shiva

and the Year Beyond

## Nechama Liss-Levinson, Ph.D.

**JEWISH LIGHTS** Publishing
Woodstock, Vermont

## To Kids Who Have Used This Book,
## from the Author Who Wrote It

## Is there anything you would like to tell me about this book?
## Please write to me at this address:

Nechama Liss-Levinson
c/o Jewish Lights Publishing
P.O. Box 237
Woodstock, VT 05091

*When a Grandparent Dies:*
*A Kid's Own Remembering Workbook for Dealing with Shiva and the Year Beyond*

2008 Fifth Printing
2005 Fourth Printing
2002 Third Printing
1997 Second Printing
1995 First Printing
© 1995 by Nechama Liss-Levinson

LIBRARY OF CONGRESS CATALOGING-IN-PUBLICATION DATA
Liss-Levinson, Nechama.
When a grandparent dies : a kid's own remembering workbook for dealing with
shiva and the year beyond / by Nechama Liss-Levinson.
p.      cm.
ISBN-13: 978-1-879045-44-6 (hardcover)
ISBN-10: 1-879045-44-3 (hardcover)
1. Mourning customs, Jewish—Juvenile literature.  2. Shivah (Jewish mourning period)—Juvenile literature.  3. Grandparents—death—psychological aspects—Juvenile literature.  4. Bereavement in children—Religious aspects—Judaism—Juvenile literature.  5. Judaism—Customs and practices—Juvenile literature.  6. Children and death—Juvenile literature.  7. Creative activities and seat work—Juvenile literature.  I. Title.
BM712.L57  1995                                              95-5379
296.4'45—dc20                                                   CIP
                                                                AC

10  9  8  7  6  5

Manufactured in China
Book and cover design: Karen Savary
Illustrations: Karen Savary

Published by Jewish Lights Publishing
A Division of LongHill Partners, Inc.
Sunset Farm Offices, Rte. 4, P.O. Box 237
Woodstock, VT 05091
Tel: (802) 457-4000    Fax: (802) 457-4004
**www.jewishlights.com**

# Contents

In loving memory of my parents,

Gertrude and Morris Joseph Liss,

also known as Grandma Bubbles and JoJo.

May remembering them be a source of blessings.

# Acknowledgments

My children, Bluma and Rivka, are the inspirations for this book. Without them, it would never have been written. They have been a great help to me, often letting me know how kids might think or feel. They bring me joy and make me laugh.

When my sisters Jaquie and Suzy and I sat *shiva* together, we shared ideas for remembering. That was the beginning of this book.

Some good friends have believed in me as a writer and have encouraged me at different points along the way. Their names are: Miriam, Jill, Meir, Carol, Mark, Helen, Harvey, Irene, Paul, George, Anne, Les, Pat, Susan, David, Harriet, Myra, Rochelle, Eleanor, Mutzie, Bracha, Larry, and George.

I was very happy when the publisher of Jewish Lights Publishing, Stuart Matlins, decided to publish this book. I want to thank him, and his warm, dependable assistant editor, Sandra Korinchak, for their faith in this idea. I also thank Seymour Rossel for his careful editing.

Finally, I want to thank my husband, Billy, whose love is the spark that lights my life. He has filled our home with humor, respect, and the encouragement to be yourself.

# What This Book Is About and How to Use It

If you are reading this book, something sad probably happened in your family. One of your grandparents died. It may have been your grandmother. It may have been your grandfather.

This is your book. Unlike other books, you can write in this one. You can draw, doodle, take notes, tape in pictures, and even fold the pages.

✎ Begin by writing the name of the person who died:

_____

You can have so many different feelings when someone dies. You might be sad, angry, mixed-up, or scared. At times, you may not feel anything at all. Your feelings might be going up and down like a roller coaster. One minute, you want to cry, and then, you just don't feel like crying. Some kids feel unexpected things, like wanting to act silly, or to laugh a lot. Sometimes, kids feel guilty for things they did, or for feelings they had about their grandparents. Some kids might feel glad that their grandparents aren't sick anymore. Some kids are worried about their parents, or about a grandparent who is still alive.

What are some of the ways you have been feeling?

_____

_____

_____

When someone you love dies, life can seem very confusing for a while. In the Jewish religion, after someone dies, there is a funeral, a special service where rabbis, friends, and family say prayers, and tell stories about the person who died. These stories told at the funeral are called a eulogy; in Hebrew, they're called a *hesped*. After the funeral, the person's body is buried. For the week following the burial, the family of the person who died has a special time to think about what has happened. This special time is called *shiva* (**shih**-vah), the Hebrew word for the number seven. It stands for seven days, the traditional time of *shiva*.

7

Sometimes, kids don't know what to do during *shiva,* and feel kind of left out or strange. Some kids who felt close to their grandparents miss them a lot, and aren't sure how to handle those feelings. Other kids didn't know their grandparents so well, and feel weird not feeling as sad as they think they should.

This book is to help you during *shiva,* and for the days and weeks and months afterward. The first part is a special section with things to do during *shiva.* The second part has activity pages you can use later on, any day of the year. And the third part can help you think about your grandparents during the Jewish holidays. You can fill out the pages in the order they're written, or you can skip around. There may be some pages you don't want to do at all. That's okay. It's up to you.

There may be a lot of questions you have about what happened, and about what's going to happen in the future. This book will help you to answer some of those questions, and to encourage you to go to your mom or dad to ask more questions. This is a book to help you in remembering your grandparent who died. As you fill in this book, you will be creating a special treasure that you can keep forever.

✎ Draw a picture of your grandparent who died. (You can draw from memory or use a photograph to help you.)

---

**My Grandparent**

---

# p a r t   o n e
## *Remembering During the First Week– Shiva*

When someone we love dies, the world may suddenly seem upside down. You don't know what to do or what to say. Our Jewish tradition helps us to feel less mixed up by giving us special instructions on "What to Do" in the week right after someone in our family dies. This section has some activities to help you during that special week called *shiva*.

# Sitting Shiva—What Does That Mean?

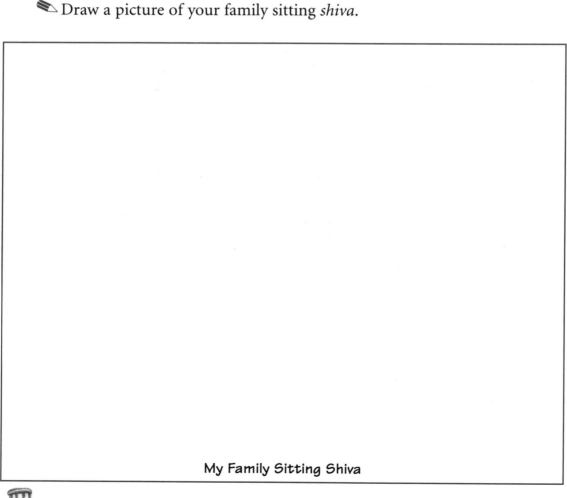

During *shiva,* families often try to spend their time together. They may stay at the home of the person who died, or in their own home. During that week, prayers are said at home, and the family has time to talk, tell stories, and give each other comforting hugs.

During *shiva,* many people may come to visit. These are the *shiva* visitors. They want to offer their love and support to the family. They also want to have some time to think about and remember the person who died.

You might hear people say that the family is "sitting *shiva.*" This is because close family members of the person who died traditionally sit on small, low chairs or on boxes during the time of *shiva.* The little chairs are supposed to make everyone remember how little you might feel when someone you love dies.

✎ Draw a picture of your family sitting *shiva.*

My Family Sitting Shiva

# The Special Prayer We Call Kaddish

During *shiva,* and for almost a whole year afterwards, it is the Jewish tradition that the children of the person who died say a special prayer every day. This prayer is called *Kaddish* (**kah**-dish). *Kaddish* is said for lots of different reasons, but there is a special "Mourner's *Kaddish*." Saying this prayer gives people a chance every day to remember the person who died.

There is something very interesting about this prayer. Even though the people who are saying it may be thinking about the person who died, the prayer does not talk about death. Instead, the prayer talks about the idea that God is very important in our lives. The prayer says that we should praise God and say that God is wonderful!

Why would we say a prayer like that now? When something bad happens in your life, it is hard to make sense of it. Sometimes, we want to blame someone else for bad things that happen. Sometimes we say, "You made me spill the juice," or "It was your fault I didn't get that ball in the basket." When someone dies, we might be angry at God, and think, "I don't like God right now, because my grandparent died"!

The *Kaddish* prayer reminds us that even when bad things happen in our life, we should try to remember all of the good things that God has created for us in this world (like just being alive, for example, or like enjoying snowflakes, roller blades, ice cream, and summer vacation).

What would you write if you were going to compose a prayer for mourners?

## My Kaddish Prayer

_____

_____

_____

_____

_____

_____

# How My Grandparent Died

The first question many *shiva* visitors ask is, "How did your grandma or grandpa die?" They are curious to know what happened. Was your grandparent sick for a long time, or for a short time? Was there an accident? What happened? If you don't know the answer, you should ask your mom or dad. If you don't understand what happened, it is okay to keep asking questions until you understand what they are saying.

Who told you that your grandparent died?

_____

What did they say?

_____

_____

_____

_____

_____

What questions do you still have?

_____

_____

_____

_____

_____

_____

_____

_____

_____

# Be a Shiva Detective

Lots of people come to visit the family during *shiva*. They come to let you know that they care about you, and about how you are feeling now. They want to offer comfort to you and your family. They often want to talk about your grandma or grandpa who died.

You may know some of the *shiva* visitors. Others may be people you'll be meeting for the first time. Some will be friends of your parents. Some will be friends of your grandparents. And some will be members of your family, like aunts and uncles, or cousins.

Sometimes, a friend may visit who knew your grandma or grandpa when he or she was your age. Sometimes, there will be a cousin who grew up with your grandma or grandpa. During *shiva*, you may hear some very interesting stories about your grandparents, stories that most people have already forgotten. Your job during *shiva* can be the "*Shiva* Detective." If you are a very good *Shiva* Detective, you may uncover some amazing clues to knowing the kind of person your grandma or grandpa was.

**Here are some questions that you might ask *shiva* visitors:**

How did you know my grandparent?

How old were you both when you met?

What do you remember about your first meeting?

What was the most fun time the two of you had together?

How would you describe my grandma or grandpa as a friend?

**Special questions for family:**

How did my grandmother and grandfather meet?

What was the wedding like?

What holidays did you spend together? What kinds of things did you do to celebrate?

What was my grandma like as a mother? as a wife, sister, cousin, aunt?

*or:*

What was my grandpa like as a father? as a husband, brother, cousin, uncle?

✎ Write down the answers to these and other questions that you think of, in the next few pages—your *Shiva* **Detective Notebook.**

 My Shiva Detective Notebook

*Shiva* Visitor's Name: _____

Relationship: _____

*Shiva* Detective's Report: _____

_____

_____

_____

_____

_____

*Shiva* Visitor's Name: _____

Relationship: _____

*Shiva* Detective's Report: _____

_____

_____

_____

_____

_____

*Shiva* Visitor's Name: _____

Relationship: _____

*Shiva* Detective's Report: _____

_____

_____

_____

_____

# 🔍 My Shiva Detective Notebook

*Shiva* Visitor's Name:_____

Relationship: _____

*Shiva* Detective's Report: _____

_____

_____

_____

_____

_____


*Shiva* Visitor's Name:_____

Relationship: _____

*Shiva* Detective's Report: _____

_____

_____

_____

_____

_____


*Shiva* Visitor's Name:_____

Relationship: _____

*Shiva* Detective's Report: _____

_____

_____

_____

_____

_____

# Shiva Detective Biography

A biography is the story of someone's life. To write your grandparent's biography, see how many blanks you can fill in.

This is a story about my grand_____. My grand_____ was born on _____ in _____.
(S)He was the _____ child in the family. (S)He had _____ brothers and _____ sisters. Her(His) parents were born in _____.
Her(His) mom spent her time _____, and her(his) dad spent his time _____.

   Growing up, my grand_____ went to school at _____.
(S)He really liked to study _____. (S)He didn't like to study _____. My grandparents met _____,
and got married on _____.
They lived in _____. They had _____
children, including my _____ who was born
on _____. As a family, they used to like
to _____. On week-
ends they used to _____.
When my (mom) (dad) was growing up, they thought my grand_____ was
really _____.

   Since I have been around in the family, my grand_____ has lived
in _____. The things I liked to do with my
grand_____ are _____
and _____. My grand_____ died
on _____.

# Names in My Family

**My Name**

✎ Write your own name in English and Hebrew.

My English Name:

_____

First Name                     Middle Name                     Last Name

My Hebrew Name: (**Shiva Detective Hint:** Start at the right!)

_____

Name                          (Start Here)

Son of / Daughter of

_____

My Dad's Hebrew Name              and              My Mom's Hebrew Name

In Judaism, our Hebrew names include our parents' names. That is, I am "Nechama Fruma, the daughter of Moshe Yosef and Gitel Tova." Your Hebrew name includes the name of your father and mother, just as your grandparent's name includes the names of his or her own father and mother, too!

Do you know whom you were named after? _____

What can you find out about the person you were named after? _____

_____

_____

_____

_____

_____

## My Grandparent's Name

✎ Now write down your grandparent's name. First, write down his or her name in English, and then in Hebrew. Get help if you need it.

My Grandparent's Name in English:

_____

First Name          Middle Name          Last Name

My Grandparent's Name in Hebrew:

_____

Name          (Start Here)

### Son of / Daughter of

_____

My Grandparent's Father      and      My Grandparent's Mother
(your great-grandfather)              (your great-grandmother)

Does your grandparent's name have a meaning? For example, the Hebrew name "Tova" means good. The English name "Pearl" describes a precious gem. Sometimes, a name has meaning because it is also the name of a hero or heroine from the Torah or later Jewish history. Esther was a famous queen who helped save the Jewish people.

Meaning of my grandparent's name: _____

_____

**Shiva Detective Job:** See if you can find out the person your grandparent was named after. Do any of the *shiva* visitors know?

My grandparent was named after _____

and this is what I found out about that person: _____

_____

_____

## What Makes Names Special

Kids have different names for their grandparents. Some people call their grandparents Grandpa Aaron, or Grandma Sylvia. Others call them by using the Hebrew words, Saba or Savta. Some people use the Yiddish words, Zayde or Bubbe. Or sometimes people have their own special words that just their family knows, like Poppey, or PopPop, or Grammie, or JoJo.

✏ On this page, write down what you called your grandma or grandpa. Sometimes there is a family story of how someone got their name. Be a *Shiva* Detective and find out why if you can!

My Special Name for My Grandparent:

_____

How They Got That Name: _____

_____

_____

_____

_____

When you say your grandparents' names, George and Helen, or Norm and Marilyn, do you think of your grandparents? Can you see a picture of them in your mind? In the Jewish tradition, sometimes people try to remember a person by naming a new baby after them. When we see the new baby, and say the baby's name out loud, it helps us remember the person who died. It's a way to keep the memory of someone you love alive. Maybe when you're older and have children of your own, you will want to name one of them after your grandmother or grandfather.

19

# My Family Tree

On the next page is a picture of a tree. It is a special kind of tree, one that shows you how all the people in your family are related to each other. For the tree to work, you need to do some *Shiva* Detective work, and fill in the branches.

Put your own name at the bottom of the page, at the place marked "me." Then see if your mom or dad, or some of the other people you speak to as *Shiva* Detective, can help you fill in the other branches of the family tree. You can add the names of any brothers or sisters you have. Now add your parents' names, and their brothers and sisters, along with your cousins.

Now you're up to your grandparents. Do you know the names of their parents? That's going back pretty far. But maybe one of the *shiva* visitors can help you with this.

**Shiva Detective Hint:** Not every family tree looks the same. In some families, someone may be widowed or divorced or remarried. This tree has lots of extra spaces so that you can fill in the branches to look like your family.

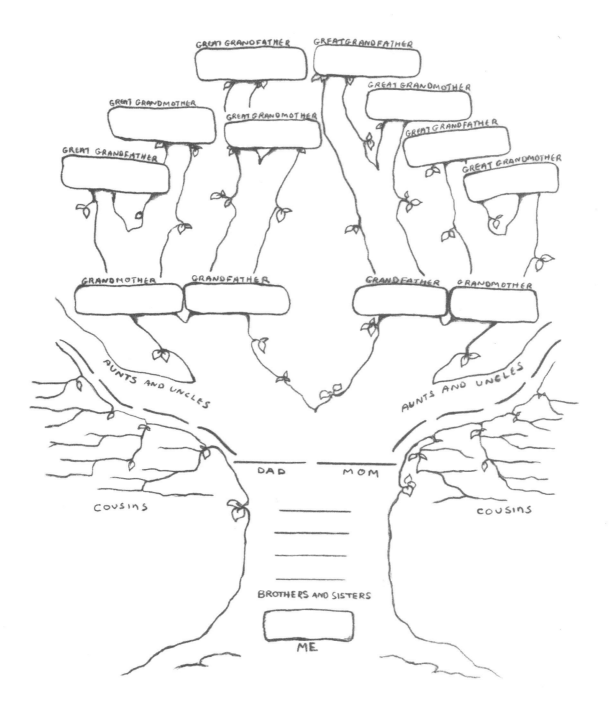

GREAT GRANDFATHER

GREAT GRANDFATHER

GREAT GRANDMOTHER

GREAT GRANDMOTHER

GREAT GRANDMOTHER

GREAT GRANDFATHER

GREAT GRANDFATHER

GREAT GRANDMOTHER

GRANDMOTHER

GRANDFATHER

GRANDFATHER

GRANDMOTHER

AUNTS AND UNCLES

AUNTS AND UNCLES

DAD

MOM

COUSINS

COUSINS

BROTHERS AND SISTERS

ME

My Family Tree

# Remembering by Giving

In the Jewish religion, we often give *tzedakah* (tse-dah-**kah**)—charity—as a way to remember and honor the memory of someone who died. Giving money to plant trees is one way you might choose to remember someone, because you are putting something living on this earth which will keep growing every year. Trees will add oxygen and beauty to the earth. The Jewish National Fund is an organization that plants trees in Israel. If you send them money to plant a tree in memory of your grandparent, they will send you a certificate with your grandparent's name on it. You can put the certificate on this page.

You might be able to think of other charities and good causes in which your grandparent would have been interested. Maybe your grandparent volunteered at a shelter to help the homeless. Or maybe he or she was interested in getting Braille books made for blind children. Your grandparent might have been involved in saving the earth or in protecting endangered animals. As a *Shiva* Detective, you can find out what interested your grandparent.

Sometimes, kids want to give money to the synagogue or temple to which their grandparents belonged. Some kids think about their grandparents, and want to give to a charity for older people who are still alive, and who need help with things like getting hot cooked meals.

You can choose a place to give *tzedakah* and send money there in memory of your grandparent. This is a very special way to remember, because you are also helping the world at the same time. The organization will send you a thank you note that you can put on this page.

> You can put a thank you note here

# Some Ideas and Addresses for Giving Tzedakah

**To plant trees in Israel**
Jewish National Fund
42 E. 69th St.
New York, NY 10021
(888) JNF-0099
www.jnf.org

**To help Jewish people worldwide**
United Jewish Communities
P.O. Box 30
Old Chelsea Station
New York, NY 10113
(212) 284-6500
www.ujc.org

**To feed the hungry**
MAZON
1990 S. Bundy Dr., Ste. 260
Los Angeles, CA 90025
(310) 442-0020
www.mazon.org

**To welcome the stranger**
Hebrew Immigrant Aid Society
(HIAS)
333 7th Ave., 16th Fl.
New York, NY 10001
(212) 967-4100
www.hias.org

**To help the homeless**
Partnership for the Homeless
305 Seventh Ave., 13th Fl.
New York, NY 10001
(212) 645-3444
www.partnershipforthehomeless.org

**To help older Jews**
Dorot
171 W. 85th St.
New York, NY 10024
(212) 769-2850
www.dorotusa.org

**To help blind and
visually impaired Jews**
Jewish Braille Institute of America
110 E. 30th St.
New York, NY 10016
(212) 889-2525
www.jewishbraille.org

**To help provide funerals
for poor Jews**
Hebrew Free Burial Association
224 W. 35th St., Room 300
New York, NY 10001
(212) 239-1662
www.hebrewfreeburial.org

**To help non-Jews who saved Jews from the Nazis**
The Jewish Foundation for
the Righteous
305 7th Ave., 19th Fl.
New York, NY 10001
(212) 727-9955
www.jfr.org

**To help very ill people and their families**
National Institute for Jewish Hospice
732 University St.
North Woodmere, New York 11581
(800) 446-4448
www.nijh.org

**To help with medical emergencies in Israel**
ARMDI: American Red Magen David
for Israel
888 7th Ave., Ste. 403
New York, NY 10106
(212) 757-1627
www.afmda.org

**To help women in need**
Jewish Women International
2000 M St. NW, Ste. 720
Washington, DC 20036
(800) 343-2823
www.jwi.org

**To remove landmines**
Campaign for a Landmine Free
World
Veterans for America
1025 Vermont Ave., NW, 7th Fl.
Washington, DC 20005
(202) 483-9222
www.veteransforamerica.org

**To help people and communities in Africa, Asia and Latin America**
American Jewish World Service
45 W. 36th St.
New York, NY 10018
(212) 792-2900
www.ajws.org

**To help endangered animals**
World Wildlife Fund
1250 24th St. NW
P.O. Box 97180
Washington, DC 20090
(202) 293-4800
www.worldwildlife.org

**For creative tzedakah projects**
Ziv Tzedakah Fund
384 Wyoming Ave.
Millburn, NJ 07041
(973) 763-9396
www.ziv.org

# p a r t   t w o

# *Remembering Throughout the Whole Year*

Even though *shiva* is over, you may still have feelings about your grandparent's death. Sometimes, you may not think about what happened for days or even weeks at a time. Then, suddenly, you remember, and feel all kinds of feelings. Our Jewish tradition gives us special ways to remember. Here are some projects to do over the coming months and year to help you when you are thinking about your grandparent.

# Photo Memories of My Grandparent

Photographs are a wonderful way to help your memory work. When you see a photo, the picture helps you to remember the people, places, and things in it. You can create a special photo album on these pages. (If you don't have a photograph for one of these memories, you can draw a picture in its place.)

## My Photo Album

- Picture of your grandparent as a child or teenager
- Favorite picture of you with your grandparent
- Recent picture of your grandparent (with or without you)
- Picture of your grandma or grandpa with your mom or dad
- Wedding picture of your grandparents
- Any other pictures you want to include

**Shiva Detective Hint:** You can ask *shiva* visitors to bring or send photos of your grandparent to you. You can also ask them to tell you the story the picture shows.

# My Photo Album

# How I Am Like My Grandparent

Do people ever look at your mom or dad and say you look just like one of them? That you have your dad's eyes? Or your mom's smile?

**How do you feel about that?**

_____

_____

_____

     There are probably certain ways that you also look like your grandma or grandpa who died. You may have the same color eyes. Or your hair may be the same color his or hers was at your age. (Hair color usually changes as we get older! Your _Shiva_ Detective talents are needed here to find out your grandparent's hair color as a child.) Maybe you can find a picture of your grandparent at a young age, and notice ways in which you might appear similar. You might like some of the ways in which you look the same, and you may not like some of them!

**Ways I Look Like My Grandparent:**

_____

_____

_____

     Perhaps even more importantly, there may be ways that you act like your grandparent, or special talents you may have gotten from them. For example, do you laugh like your grandma? Are you a good tennis player, like your grandpa? Do you find math really easy at school, like Grandma always did? Do you have a fantastic memory, like Grandpa?

**Ways I Act Like My Grandparent:**

_____

_____

_____

So far, we've looked at features and talents you inherited from your grandparent, like having brown eyes, or being good at drawing. You can't really choose the ways that you look like someone, or even the special talents you inherit from them. But there are other ways you can choose to be like someone you admire or love. For example, you can be generous and give money to *tzedakah*, as you know a grandparent did. You can read many books, just as he or she did. You can be a loyal friend. You can recycle things to help the environment. It's a very special compliment to choose to be like someone.

**A Way I Choose to Be Like My Grandparent:**

_____

_____

_____

_____

## Complaints Department

This part may be a little difficult to do. When someone dies, we usually think about all the terrific things we remember about that person. However, all of us sometimes think about things we just didn't like about someone. Sometimes, you think someone talks too loudly. Sometimes, you think someone has a funny smell. Sometimes, you feel someone always criticizes you. Just like we can think about ways we want to be like our grandparents, we can also think about some ways we wouldn't want to be like them. This is a page for you to be able to write out your complaints. If you want it to be private, you can fold the page over when you are finished writing it.

**Some Things I Didn't Like about My Grandparent:**

_____

_____

_____

_____

# My Grandparent's Gravestone

After someone dies, their body is buried in a grave at a special kind of park, called a cemetery. Many, many people are buried at the same cemetery. You need some kind of permanent sign to know where the person you love is buried. That sign, which marks the spot of your grandma or grandpa's grave, is called a gravestone. In Hebrew, the gravestone is called a *matzevah* (mah-tseh-**vah**).

Usually, Jewish families set up the gravestone sometime during the year after the funeral. Most gravestones include the person's name in English and Hebrew, and the dates that they were born and died. Sometimes, other things are added: a Jewish symbol, like a menorah or a Jewish star, words to describe the person, like "loving grandma" or "darling wife." Sometimes people add a sentence, or even a poem, which describes the person, like "She made everyone laugh."

The *matzevah* is usually made out of a large stone, and an artist carves the words or pictures right into the stone. The family of the person who died designs the gravestone and orders it from a special factory, where they are made. Using the sample here, see if you can design a gravestone on the next page for your grandparent. Put in the name and the dates of birth and death. Then decide what other things you want to add. See if there is a picture you want to draw, or a few words which describe  your grandparent. Maybe you can share your ideas, and be a helper when it comes time to order the actual gravestone for your grandma or grandpa.

My Design for My Grandparent's Matzevah

# The Unveiling of the Gravestone

Sometime during the first year after a person dies, the family and closest friends come to the cemetery to see the new gravestone, and to remember the person who died. Before the family arrives at the cemetery, the rabbi covers the gravestone with a piece of cloth so that nobody gets to see it first. Then, when everyone arrives, the piece of cloth is taken off, and the new gravestone is unveiled. That is why this ceremony is called the "unveiling."

At the unveiling a few prayers are said, including the Mourner's *Kaddish*. In addition, sometimes people tell stories about the person who died. After the unveiling, whenever you visit the cemetery, it is the custom to pick up a small stone or pebble and put it on the gravestone. It is a sign in Jewish tradition that someone came to visit the person in this grave, and that this person is remembered.

For the unveiling, you may wish to write down some of your own thoughts about your grandparent. One way to do this is to pretend you are writing a letter to him or her. If you want to, you can share your letter with your family at the unveiling.

Date_____

Dear _____ ,

There's a lot I've been thinking about since you died. _____

_____

_____

_____

_____

_____

_____

_____

_____

Love,

_____

# A Special Time for Remembering We Call Yahrzeit

You may remember for a long time the day that your grandparent died. When that day or season comes around, you might especially think of the person who died.

**The Date My Grandparent Died:** _____

In addition to the regular or "civil" calendar (with months like January, February, etc.), we have a Jewish calendar. Every day on the civil calendar also has a date on the Jewish calendar. The anniversary of the Hebrew date that someone died is called the *yahrzeit* (**yar**-tsite).

See if you can find out the *yahrzeit* date for your grandparent. You will need a Jewish calendar. You can check with your family's rabbi. You can check with someone at the funeral chapel. Somebody will know.

(**Shiva Detective Hint:** Remember, in the Jewish religion, the date starts in the evening. So if somebody died after sunset, it is considered as though they died on the next Hebrew day.)

**My Grandparent's *Yahrzeit:*** _____
Hebrew Date

Every year, we do things to remember the person who died on the date of his or her *yahrzeit*. We may go with our family to the synagogue to say the *Kaddish* prayer. We may light a special candle in memory of him or her. This *yahrzeit* candle burns for twenty-four hours—the whole night and day. We may again give charity in memory of our grandparent, and talk about him or her. The *yahrzeit* date is always the same Hebrew date, but it will jump around a bit on the civil calendar.

Now see if you can find out the civil calendar date for your grandparent's *yahrzeit* for the coming years. You may need some help from your rabbi.

✎ Write down the civil date for the *yahrzeit* in the coming years. It is a special date for you to remember.

## The Civil Date of the *Yahrzeit:*

In 20__: _____    In 20__: _____

In 20__: _____    In 20__: _____

In 20__: _____    In 20__: _____

In 20__: _____    In 20__: _____

# Shiva Detective Mind Benders

✎ With all you discovered about your grandparent in your detective work, try to complete the following sentences.

My best time with my grandparent was_____

_____

Having my grandparent die makes me think about _____

_____

I loved it when my grandparent_____

_____

If I could have one thing that belonged to my grandparent, I would choose _____

_____

The way my mom or dad is just like my grandparent is_____

_____

Since my grandparent died, I sometimes worry about _____

_____

The one thing I wish my grandparent could do with me now is _____

_____

The one thing I'm most upset about my grandparent not being able to do with me is

_____

My grandparent taught me something about _____

_____

When I'm a grandparent, I would like to _____

_____

Something my grandparent always used to say was _____

_____

# p a r t   t h r e e

# *Remembering During the Holidays*

Celebrating the holidays can be fun. We do special things for each holiday, like asking the "Four Questions" on Passover, dipping apples in honey on Rosh Hashanah (rohsh hah-shah-nah), and lighting candles for Shabbat (shah-**baht**). Holiday times can make us feel closer to our families. But we might also feel sad when we remember and miss people who have died. Here are some ideas for ways to keep the memory of your grandparent alive as part of your holiday celebration.

# The Taste of Shabbat

There is an old Jewish story about a Russian general who came to eat dinner at the house of his Jewish friend on Friday night. He loved everything he had for dinner. A few days later, the general sent his servant over to get the recipes for the *challah* (hah-**lah**), the gefilte fish, the chicken, the sweet noodle pudding with apples and raisins, and the chocolate fudge pie. But when all these foods were made at the general's house, they didn't taste the same. "Why didn't you give me the real recipes?" the general asked. "I did," said his Jewish friend. "But one thing was missing. You didn't include the special 'taste of Shabbat.' Only when you think about Shabbat while you make the food will the food taste as good as it did last Friday night."

Often, we remember sharing good times with people at holiday meals and celebrations we had together. Maybe you remember Grandpa's special "Chicken à la Grandpa," or Grandma's famous spaghetti with tomato sauce. Maybe you remember the French toast Grandpa made when you would come to visit, or Grandma's chocolate chip cookies.

See if you can get the recipe for one or two of your favorite dishes that your grandma or grandpa made. You can try to make them yourself, or maybe your mom or dad will help you. In any case, when you make the special food, and then again, when you eat it, have a special thought about your grandparent. This is like the "taste of Shabbat," the secret ingredient you can add to the recipe to make it taste as delicious as when your grandma or grandpa made it.

**Shiva Detective Note:** Maybe your grandparent didn't cook at all. But he or she may have taken you out to a restaurant, or maybe to a bakery to get a cupcake or a cookie. You can write down something that you liked eating when you were together, and then, with some help, you can find a recipe for that food.

Special Recipe for:_____

**Ingredients:**

_____
_____
_____
_____

**Directions:**

_____
_____
_____
_____
_____
_____
_____
_____
_____

**My memories of Grandma or Grandpa making this recipe:**

_____
_____
_____
_____
_____
_____
_____

# Rosh Hashanah

When you think of *Rosh Hashanah,* what do you think of?

_____

_____

Do you think about dipping apples in honey for a sweet new year? Do you think about hearing the loud sounds of the *shofar*? Do you think of families getting together saying "Happy New Year" to each other? Did you get together with your grandparents for *Rosh Hashanah*? If so, it will feel different this year.

On *Rosh Hashanah,* we think about our lives over the past year. One of the things we think about is how we have treated other people. We often want a chance to say we're sorry, and to figure out how to act differently in the future. One of the hardest things in life is feeling we acted badly toward someone who died before we had a chance to say we were sorry. Almost everyone can think about something they wish they had done a little differently. Perhaps you wish you had called your grandma or grandpa more often on the telephone. Maybe you two had a fight just before he or she died. You think of things you wish you had said or done, but now it seems too late. This can feel pretty upsetting for kids and adults alike. Sometimes, you feel guilty.

It's important to know that almost everyone has feelings like that. Nobody is perfect as a son or daughter, or as a grandson or granddaughter, or even as a mom or dad, or a grandma or grandpa. Still, it's important to have a chance to think about your behavior, and make plans for how you want to make changes for the future. Here are some ideas, step by step:

**1.** Write a list of things you may have done wrong or things for which you would like to apologize to your grandparent. Some may be little things. Some may seem like big things.

**Things I'm Sorry About**

A._____

B._____

C._____

# Tashlich

✎ **2.** Next to each item on the list, see if you can figure out why you acted the way you did. For example, if you didn't call your grandmother as much as you think you should have, was there some reason? Maybe you found it a little hard to find things to talk about? Maybe you thought she criticized you a lot? Talk to your parents. Maybe they can tell you something about your grandparent that will help you to understand your feelings and actions. Usually, there is some meaning to the way we behave.

**Why I Acted That Way**

A._____

B._____

C._____

All of us know of things we have done in the past year that we don't like very much. We were mean to our sister or brother. We were grumpy with our parents. We left out a friend. We think about these actions on *Rosh Hashanah.* However, we also get a chance to do something about our past actions. There is a Jewish ceremony for the afternoon of *Rosh Hashanah,* when we can throw away all the bad things we have done. We get rid of them along with the bad feelings that go with them.

This ceremony is called *tashlich* (**tahsh**-likh). We go with our friends and our family to a place where there is water. Maybe there is a little pond near your house. Or maybe there is a river, or even an ocean. Usually we bring little bags with us, filled with bread crumbs. The bread crumbs stand for our bad actions from the past year. We throw them into the water, letting the fish or the birds gobble them up. We say a prayer about wanting to change the ways we sometimes act. We try to imagine that we are throwing away our bad actions.

This year, on *Rosh Hashanah,* you might add something extra to the *tashlich* ceremony. Remember the list of the "Things I'm Sorry About"? Copy that list onto a piece of paper, and tear it into little tiny pieces. Take those pieces with you to *tashlich.* When you get to the water, try to speak to your memory of your grandparent. Tell them what you're sorry about. Maybe you'll feel like he or she can hear you in some way; maybe you won't. Try doing it anyway. Then, throw the pieces of paper into the water, along with the bread crumbs.

Good-bye, good-bye to those things!

41

# Yom Kippur

*Yom Kippur* (yohm kih-**poor**) is a time to make changes. There is a special Jewish way to help us change our lives. This way is called *teshuvah* (t'shoo-**vah**). We can turn our lives around by following three simple steps.

1. We think of what we have done wrong, and feel truly sorry for it.

2. We tell the person we have hurt that we are sorry.

3. We think about how to act differently, and when a similar situation comes up again, we act in a new and different way.

✎ **3.** You have already done steps 1 and 2 in doing *teshuvah*. Now, it's time for step 3, making changes. Think about what you've learned about how you acted, and see if there's a way you would like to change for the future. For example, if you were always too busy to call your grandfather, is there a way that you can now remind yourself to call someone else who is important to you?

## Some Ideas on How I'm Going to Act Differently

A._____

_____

_____

B._____

_____

_____

C._____

_____

_____

# Hanukkah

A lot of kids say that *Hanukkah* (hah-nuh-**kah**) is one of their favorite Jewish holidays. Most kids like getting presents on *Hanukkah*. They like to have parties with their friends and family. They like eating *latkes* (potato pancakes) and playing *dreidel*. Now that your grandparent has died, this Hanukkah may seem a little different.

Think about a special present that you got in the past from your grandparent. Was it a bicycle, a book, a doll, a computer program?

_____

*A special* Hanukkah *present from my grandparent*

Now think again. Your grandparent may have given you another kind of gift, not one that can be bought in a store. For example, maybe you took a special trip with your grandma. Or maybe you and your grandpa had a special day at the beach together. Or maybe there was a special song, or story, or way that they hugged you, or understood how you felt when you were sad. See if you can remember a special gift that you got from your grandparent. This gift is one that you can't touch and that you can't buy in a store, but one that you can keep in your heart.

_____

*A special gift from my grandparent I can't buy in a store*

43

*Hanukkah* celebrates the story of how a small number of Jewish people won many battles against the powerful Syrian army. The fight was hard, but the Jewish people kept at it until they won. Each of us sometimes has to work really hard to deal with a problem in our lives.

Speak to your parents to find out if there was some way in which your grandparent had to do something hard in his or her life, for example, coming to America from another country, overcoming a physical problem, or raising a family with very little money. Write your own grandparent's personal *Hanukkah* story—how your grandparent fought and won a victory in his or her life.

### My Grandparent's *Hanukkah* Story

_____

_____

_____

_____

_____

_____

_____

_____

_____

_____

# Pesach—A Time for Passover Questions

Passover is a Jewish celebration when most families get together. In Hebrew it is called *Pesach* (**peh**-sakh). Do you go to someone's house or do guests come to your home for the *Seder* (**say**-dur)? Were you often with your grandparents for your *Seder*? If you were, this might be a time that you miss them very much.

At the *Seder,* there are lots and lots of questions. The youngest child asks "The Four Questions." And if you look into the *Haggadah* (hah-gah-**dah**), you will see many more questions, including the song near the end of the *Seder,* "Who Knows One?"

When somebody dies, they can't answer our questions anymore. What questions would you like to ask your grandparent, if you could? See if you can come up with four questions for your grandma or grandpa.

**My Four Questions**

1. _____

_____

2. _____

_____

3. _____

_____

4. _____

_____

**Shiva Detective Job:** Now, see if you can guess how your grandparent would answer the questions. Or speak to your mom or dad. Maybe they'll know the answer to the questions. Or maybe, because they knew their own mom or dad, they'll be able to tell you what they think your grandma or grandpa would have said.

# Remembering My Grandparent in the Circle of Life

This circle stands for the earth, which keeps turning around and around every day of the week, month after month, year after year. As time goes on, our feelings may also go around. Sometimes, memories that used to make us feel sad now bring us happiness.

Everything has its season, and there is a time for every

be sad and a time to dance... (Ecclesiastes 3:1-2,4)

thing under the heavens. A time to be born, and a time to die... A time to cry and a time to laugh... A time to

Inside this circle, you can make a collage celebrating your grandparent's life. You can draw, paint, cut out pictures or words from magazines, paste in photographs, pieces of ribbon, wrapping paper, or any other materials you can think of.

# Glossary

**Bubbe:** Yiddish word for grandmother

**Cemetery:** Special area of land, which looks like a park, set aside for burial of the dead

**Challah:** Traditional bread for *Shabbat* meals

**Dreidel:** *Hanukkah* toy, like a spinning top

**Eulogy:** The stories about a person's life which are told at the funeral service; called *hesped* in Hebrew

**Funeral:** Service which takes place after a person dies, where friends and family gather to say prayers and tell stories about the life of the person who died

**Haggadah:** Special Jewish book used during the *Seder* meal on the holiday of Passover

**Hanukkah:** Jewish holiday celebrated for eight days in the winter, celebrating religious freedom

**Hanukkiah** (sometimes called *menorah*): Special candelabra (candle holder) for *Hanukkah,* with places for nine candles, one candle for each night and a ninth candle to light the others

**Kaddish:** Jewish prayer praising God, said on many occasions, and often said when remembering someone who died

**Latkes:** Potato pancakes; traditional food eaten on the holiday of *Hanukkah*

**Menorah:** Special candelabra (candle holder) used in the temple in Jerusalem in ancient times

**Matzevah:** Gravestone or marker to show the place where someone is buried

**Passover:** Jewish holiday of freedom in the spring, when we remember the Jewish people leaving Egypt, called *Pesach* in Hebrew

**Rosh Hashanah:** Jewish New Year celebration, which takes place in the fall

**Saba:** Hebrew word for grandfather

**Savta:** Hebrew word for grandmother

**Seder:** Special ceremony and meal for Passover, the Jewish holiday of freedom, when we remember God taking the Jewish people out of slavery in Egypt

**Shabbat:** Sabbath holiday, which comes every week, lasting from Friday at sunset to Saturday night when three stars come out

**Shiva:** Hebrew word for the number seven, which refers to the seven days after someone is buried, when the family has time to be together and think about the person who died

**Shofar:** Special musical instrument, made from a ram's horn, and blown on the holidays of *Rosh Hashanah* and *Yom Kippur*

**Tashlich:** Ceremony on *Rosh Hashanah* afternoon, when you go to the water, and "throw away" your bad actions and feelings from last year

**Teshuvah:** Hebrew word which means "turn around," and is the way that we can turn around our bad behaviors into good ones

**Torah:** Holy scroll of the Jewish people, containing the Five Books of Moses; the first five books of the Bible

**Tzedakah:** Charity. Giving money or time to help other people

**Unveiling:** Ceremony when the family sees a relative's gravestone at the cemetery for the first time

**Yahrzeit:** Anniversary of the Hebrew date that someone died

**Yiddish:** Jewish language spoken mainly in Europe—a mixture of Hebrew and German

**Yom Kippur:** Jewish holiday, soon after *Rosh Hashanah,* when we recall how we acted in the past year, and how we want to act in the future; also called the Day of Atonement

**Zayde:** Yiddish word for grandfather